Christmas Comfort

Christmas Comfort

Jeffrey R. Holland

BOOKCRAFT
Salt Lake City, Utah

Copyright © 1996 by Jeffrey R. Holland

All rights reserved. No part of this book may be reproduced in any form or by any means without permission in writing from the publisher, Bookcraft, Inc., 2405 W. Orton Circle, West Valley City, Utah 84119.

Bookcraft is a registered trademark of Bookcraft, Inc.

ISBN 1-57008-294-4

Third Printing, 1998

Printed in the United States of America

The second chapter of Luke provides the text for many of the great stories of Christmas. My text is taken from those sacred verses, but the passage I have in mind is not a verse we often hear at this happy season of the year. Nevertheless, I believe it is at the heart of the Christmas message.

I speak of a beautiful moment, approximately forty days after Mary's delivery of the child, when she and Joseph took the baby named Jesus to the temple, where the infant was to be presented unto the Lord. It was desirable for all children to be so presented in the temple, but in the Israelite tradition it was of particular importance to present the firstborn son, a rite stemming from the miraculous days of salvation in Egypt when the firstborn of the Israelite families were spared destruction. In memorial all firstborn sons were thereafter dedicated to the service of the Lord, including Levitical service in the temple. It was not practical for every firstborn son to be presented in the temple, let alone to render service there; nevertheless the eldest son in a family was still claimed as the Lord's own in a special way and had to be formally exempted from his requirement by the paying of an offering of redemption.

It is here that we realize just how poor Joseph and Mary were. The standard offering on behalf of such a child was a yearling lamb and a pigeon or turtledove. But in cases of severe poverty the law of Moses allowed the substitution of a second dove in place of the more expensive lamb. Mary and Joseph presented their son to his true Father that day with an offering of two turtledoves. This young couple, and this son who would save us, all knew what it was like to face economic privation at Christmastime.

As they made their way toward the temple that day, the Holy Spirit was resting upon a beloved elderly man named Simeon, one whom the scriptures describe as "just and devout." It was revealed to this gentle and venerable man that he would not die before seeing the Messiah—"the Lord's Christ," as Luke phrases it. The Spirit then led him to the temple, where he saw a young carpenter and his even younger wife enter the sanctuary with a newborn babe cradled in his mother's arms.

Simeon, who had waited all his life for "the consolation of Israel," took that consolation in his arms, praised God, and said:

> Lord, now lettest thou thy servant depart in peace, according to thy word:
> For mine eyes have seen thy salvation,
> Which thou hast prepared before the face of all people;
> A light to lighten the Gentiles, and the glory of thy people Israel.
> And Joseph and his mother marvelled at those things which were spoken of him.
> And Simeon blessed them, and said unto Mary his mother, Behold, this child is set for the fall and rising again of many in Israel; and for a sign which shall be spoken against;
> (Yea, a sword shall pierce through thy own soul also,) that the thoughts of many hearts may be revealed. (Luke 2:29–35.)

There is a profound Christmas message in the one this dear old man gave to sweet and pure Mary in that first Christmas season. He was joyously happy. He had lived to see the Son of God be born. He had held the child in his very arms. He could now die the happiest man in all of Jerusalem, maybe in all the world. But his joy was not of the superficial kind. It was not without its testing and trying. In that sense it didn't have much to do with toys or trinkets or tinsel, though these have their Christmas place. No, his joy had something to do with "the fall and rising again of many in Israel," and with this child's life—or at least his death—which would be like a sword piercing through his beloved mother's soul. We might well ask, "Was such an ominous warning, such a fateful prophecy, appropriate in this season of joy? Surely such was untimely, even unseemly, at *that* moment—when the Son of God was so young and tender and safe, and his mother so thrilled with his birth and his beauty?"

Our answer is, yes, it was appropriate *and* important. I submit that unless we see *all* the meaning and joy of Christmas the way old Simeon saw it all (and in a sense forced Joseph and Mary to see it)—the whole of Christ's life, the profound mission, the end as well as the beginning—then Christmas will be just another day off work, with food and fun and football for many and a measure of personal loneliness and family sorrow for others. *The true meaning, the unique and lasting and joyous meaning of the birth of this baby, would be in the life he would lead and especially in his death, in his triumphant atoning sacrifice (remember why Joseph and Mary are in the temple), in his prison-bursting resurrection.*

It is the life at the *other* end of the manger scene

that gives this moment of nativity in Bethlehem its ultimate meaning. Special as this child was and divine as was his conception, without that day of salvation wherein he would gain an everlasting victory over death and hell on behalf of every man, woman, and child who would ever be born—until *that* day should come, this baby's life and mission would not be complete. Worse yet, without that triumphant atonement and resurrection he might have been remembered only as one born in abject poverty, scorned in his own native village, and tortured to death by a ruthless Roman regime that knew everything about torture and death.

But wise old Simeon understood all of this—that the birth was ultimately for the death—and it thrilled his soul that salvation was come. Thus Christmas was sobering as well as sweet for him, and so too will most Christmases be for us. Lying among those gifts of gold, frankincense, and myrrh were also a crown of thorns, a makeshift royal robe, and a Roman spear.

I do not want this to be an unhappy message—indeed, I intend it to be a supremely joyful message, a message of special comfort. But to make it that I must speak of Christmases (and many other days in our individual and collective lives) that for whatever reason may not be very happy or seem to be "the season to be jolly."

For many people in many places this may not be an entirely happy Christmas, one not filled with complete joy because of the circumstances facing a spouse or a friend, a child or a grandchild. Or perhaps that was the case another Christmas in another year, but one which brings a painful annual memory to us yet. Or (and may heaven bless us that this *not* be so) perhaps this may be the case some future Christmas when, unexpectedly and undeservedly, something goes terribly wrong, when there is some public or very personal tragedy in which it may seem, at least for a time, that "hate is strong and mocks the song of peace on earth, good will to men."

By way of illustration let me share a few examples that I pray are not too painful or too personal for anyone who reads this. I recall that some years ago, in the very heart of the holiday season, a fire broke out on a conveyor belt five thousand feet into the Wilberg Mine near Orangeville in Emery County, Utah. The story gripped the entire state and drew national attention. One man miraculously escaped, but all twenty-seven of the others had finally been found or declared dead by Sunday, December 23—two days before Christmas. On Monday, December 24, an article in the *Deseret News* began: "[Today] in church, watching his mother sob, Chris Pugliese knew that this Christmastime is [going to be] different. His mother, Kathy, lost no one in the Wilberg Mine fire, but she, like others, feels the pain of those who did. Chris may not quite understand that the sadness that dampened his family's Christmas destroyed the holiday joy of twenty-seven other families. Those families may never again celebrate Christmas without recalling the death of a father, son, daughter or brother."

More recently a tragedy struck even a little closer to our family. Exactly one week before Christmas in 1994—a Sunday morning—a freak accident on Highway 128 nine miles northeast of Moab plunged four teenagers to their deaths in the frigid water of the Colorado River. They were magnificent young people by every standard—a student body president and valedictorian, two Eagle Scouts, a Laurel class president—traveling that morning to sing at a missionary friend's homecoming in nearby Castle Valley. Two of the four were brothers, Joseph and Gary

Welling, exemplary sons of our childhood friend and twenty-year St. George schoolmate, Elaine Fawson Welling. This Christmas won't be as difficult for the Welling and Stewart and Adair families as that year, but it will be difficult. It will reopen a deep wound, and every Christmas for the rest of their lives will undoubtedly carry some echo of that pain and those family memories.

May I be even a bit more personal and in conclusion leave you with something more cheerful than all of this has been so far.

On the evening of December 23, 1976, my father underwent surgery to relieve the effect of osteoarthritis in the vertebrae of his back. The surgery was successful, but near the conclusion of it he suffered a major heart attack. Eight hours later he suffered another one. From those two attacks he sustained massive damage to a heart that was already defective from an illness suffered in his youth. By the time we finally got to see him, wired and tubed and grey and unconscious, it was mid-morning on December 24, Christmas Eve. "Magnificent timing," I muttered to no one in particular.

Pat and I stayed at his side all day, as much for my mother's sake as for my father's. He was not going to live, and at age sixty she had never had to confront that possibility in their entire married life. As evening came along, we took her to our home. She needed calming and our three little children deserved some kind of Christmas Eve. Pat has created a wonderful world of holiday traditions in our family, and we tried to do the Christmas Eve portion of those, but it was a pretty joyless exercise. We tried to laugh and sing, but all that these children understood was that their grandmother was crying, their dad was very sad, and their grandfather was somewhere alone in a hospital, not free for the Christmas visit that had been planned. After hanging just a few of their mother's annual Christmas Eve gingerbread men, they uncharacteristically suggested that perhaps they should just go to bed a little early this year, reassuring everyone that this was their choice and something they really wanted to do. You can imagine how convincing they sounded. About as convincing as our caroling had been.

I gave my mother a blessing and convinced her to try to get some sleep. I stayed with Pat for a while, putting out a Christmas gift or two; then I told her to hold the family together—as she has done all of our married life—and I was going back to the hospital. There was obviously nothing I could do there. She knew it and I knew it, but she also knew it was my Santa Claus who was lying alone with all those tubes, IVs, and monitors, and she said not a word to try to get me to remain.

At the hospital I sat and walked and read and walked and looked in on Dad and walked. He would not, in fact, recover from all this. I suppose everyone knew that, but the nursing staff were kind to me and gave me free access to him and to the entire hospital. A couple of the nurses wore Santa Claus hats, and all the nursing stations were decorated for the season. During the course of the evening I think I checked them all out, and sure enough, on every floor and in every wing it was Christmas.

You will forgive me if I admit that somewhere in the early hours of the morning I was feeling pretty sorry for myself. "Why does it have to be like this?" I thought. "Why does it have to be on Christmas?" Of all the times to lose your dad, did it have to be the night when dads are the greatest guys in the world and gifts for little boys somehow appear that, in later years, would be recognized to be well beyond the meager Holland budget? Lying under that oxygen tent was the most generous man I have ever known, a Kris Kringle to end all Kris Kringles, and by some seemingly cruel turn of cardiac fate he was in the process of dying on Christmas morning. In my self-pity it did not seem right to me, and I confess I was muttering something of that aloud as I walked what surely must have been every square inch of the public (and a fair portion of the private) space in that hospital.

Then and there—2:00 or 3:00 A.M. in a very quiet hospital, immersed as I was in some sorrow and too much selfishness—heaven sent me a small, personal, pre-packaged revelation, a tiny Christmas declaration that was as powerful as any I have ever received. In the midst of mumbling about the very poor calendaring in all of this, I heard the clear, unbroken cry of a baby. It truly startled me. I had long since ceased paying attention to where I was wandering that night, and only then did I realize I was in the maternity ward; somewhere, I suppose, near the nursery. To this day I do not know just where that baby was or how I heard it. I like to think it was a brand-new baby taking that first breath and announcing that he or she had arrived in the world, the fact of which everyone was supposed to take note.

It may have just been a baby saying it was time to eat, and wondering where that comforting cuddle from a mother was. But wherever and whoever it was, God could not have sent me a more penetrating wake-up call.

I felt a little like another who, in reply to his questions, heard the Lord declare, "Who is this that darkeneth counsel by words without knowledge?" (Job 38:2.) It was as if he were saying: "Listen, Jeffrey Roy, this is the happiest night in the whole wide world for some young couple who may otherwise be poor as church mice. Maybe this is their first baby. Maybe he or she is their own personal 'consolation in Israel,' perhaps the only consolation they have right now in what may otherwise be a difficult life. In any case they love this baby, and the baby already loves them. And think of the calendaring—born on Christmas Day! What a reminder that they have each other now and forever! Whatever happens, good times or bad, they have each other. Whatever pain may lie ahead, whatever sword might pierce their souls from time to time, they will be triumphant because the Prince of Peace was also born this same day 'once in royal David's city.'

"Temporary separation at death and the other difficulties that attend us as we all move toward that end are part of the price we pay for love in this world, the price we pay for the joy of birth and family ties and the fun of Christmas together. Old Simeon, weathered and tried and tested Simeon, had it right. And so did the morning stars and the shepherds and the angels who shouted for joy, praising God and singing, 'Glory to God in the highest, and on earth peace, good will toward men.'

"Jeff, my boy," he seemed to say with that baby's cry, "I expected a little more from you. If you can't remember why all of this matters, then your pitiful approach to Christmas is no more virtuous than the over-commercialization everyone laments these days. You need to shape up just a little, to put your theology where your Christmas carols are. You can't separate Bethlehem from Gethsemane or the hasty flight into Egypt from the slow journey to the summit of Calvary. It's of one piece. It is a single plan. It considers 'the fall and rising again of many in Israel,' but always in that order. Christmas is joyful not because it is a season or decade or lifetime without pain and privation, but precisely because life does hold those moments for us. And that baby, my son, my own beloved and *Only* Begotten Son in the flesh, born 'away in a manger, [with] no crib for his bed,' makes all the difference in the world, all the difference in time and eternity, all the difference everywhere, worlds without number, a lot farther than your feeble eye can see."

I can't fully describe to you what happened to me that early yuletide morning, but it was one of the most revelatory Christmas experiences I have ever had. And it dawned on me that that could have been my young parents who were so happy that morning. I was a December baby, and my mother never wearied of telling me that that was her happiest Christmas ever.

Perhaps the joy they felt that day at my birth was to be inextricably, inseparably, eternally linked with my sorrow at their passing—that we could never expect to have the one without the other. It came to me in a profound way that in this life no one can have real love without eventually dealing with real loss, and we certainly can't rejoice over one's birth and the joy of living unless we are prepared to understand and accommodate and accept with some grace the inevitability—including the untimeliness—of difficulty and trouble and death. These are God's gifts to us—birth and life and death and salvation, the whole divine experience in all its richness and complexity.

So there lay my dad, the great gift-giver, he who found bicycles and BB guns and presents of every kind *somewhere*. Now he was making his way out of the world on Christmas Day on the wings of the greatest gift ever given. I thought of another Father. "For God so loved the world, that he gave his only begotten Son, that whosoever believeth in him should not perish, but have everlasting life" (John 3:16). True fathers and mothers were all alike, I realized; coming up with the best gifts imaginable at what is often terrible personal cost—and I am obviously *not* speaking of material gifts or monetary costs.

So I was mildly but firmly rebuked that night—by the cry of a newborn baby. I got a little refresher course in the plan of salvation and a powerful reminder of why this *is* "the season to be jolly," and why any Christmas is a time of comfort, whatever our circumstances may be. In the same breath I was also reminded that life will not always be as cozy as "chestnuts roasting on an open fire" or an unending splendor while we stroll, "walking in a winter wonderland." No, life will have its valleys and peaks, its moments for the fall and rising in the lives of all of God's children. So now it is old Simeon's joyful embrace of that little baby just before his own death that is one of the images I try to remember at Christmas.

I have repented since that night. In fact, I did some repenting there in the maternity ward. If you have to lose your dad, what more comforting time than Christmas? None of us would want those experiences for the Wilberg Mine families or the Moab seminary students or a thousand other painful experiences some people have at Christmas; but even so, in the end it is all right. It is okay. These are sad experiences, terribly wrenching experiences, with difficult moments for years and years to come. But because of the birth in Bethlehem and what it led to they are *not* tragic experiences. They have a happy ending. There is a rising after the falling. There is life always. New births and rebirths and resurrection to eternal life. It is the joy of the stable—the maternity ward—forever.

"If thou hadst been here, my brother had not

died," Martha said to him once, probably in the same tone of voice I had been using up and down the hallways of the hospital. "If that arthritis just had not required surgery, there wouldn't have been any strain on his heart. If that conveyer belt had just been shifted a little, it wouldn't have started that fire. If there just hadn't been a small patch of ice on that particular stretch of road so close to the Colorado River. . . ." And on and on and on. Jesus has one answer for us all—one answer to all the "whys" and "what ifs," all the "would haves" and "could haves" and "should haves" of our journey.

Looking sweet Martha firmly in the eyes, he said for all in Salt Lake and Orangeville and Moab to hear: "I am the resurrection, and the life; he that believeth in me, though he were dead, yet shall he live: and whosoever liveth and believeth in me shall never die" (John 11:21, 25–26).

Yes, for me the most important Christmas visitor of all may have been old Simeon, who, not in the absence of hard days and long years but because of them, would sing with us tonight at the top of his voice, "Joy to the world, the Lord is come; let earth receive her King! . . . No more will sin and sorrow grow, nor thorns infest the ground; he'll come and make the blessings flow, far as the curse was found." Of this witness I am a witness. In the name of Jesus Christ, amen.